Amazing Animals

Jozua Douglas & Loes Riphagen

Clavis

NEW YORK

There are a lot of animals in the world and you can see some of them in your own yard. There are slow snails, strong ants, and quick dragonflies. Backyards are home to cats, butterflies and birds, mice, moles, worms and beetles. The creatures crawl and crunch, they dig and sniff. How many do you see here?

There are many more animals that live in the wild. Big, small, fast, lazy, strong, beautiful, and dangerous animals.

The biggest

The biggest animal on our planet is the whale.
Whales can be as big as five houses in a row.
When a whale opens his mouth, a school bus can
easily fit into it. An animal that big has to eat a lot!
Whales like to eat little water animals like crabs,
small lobsters, and little fish. Every day a whale will
eat so many tiny animals that they could fill
a swimming pool.

The smallest

Among the creatures that mak[e]
up whale food swim the smalle[st]
animals on earth. They are call[ed]
zooplankton and are so tiny tha[t]
you can't even see them. Mor[e]
than a million of them could fi[t]
on the top of your little finger[.]

Did you know that whales talk with each other by singing? They make a sound that can be heard from far away. Whale songs can be louder than the sound of a jet plane.

The tallest

The tallest animal in the world is the giraffe. Giraffes can grow as tall as a house. That's very useful when eating dinner. With their long necks, giraffes can easily reach the leaves at the tops of the tree. But being so tall can also be tricky. When giraffes want to drink, they can't just bend down, they have to spread their legs out to the side. That can be really awkward.

Did you know

that ants have their own pets? Ants love small insects called aphids because they produce a sweet drink that the ants find delicious.

The longest

Snakes can be very long. Do you want to know how long the longest snake in the world is? Then ask fifteen children to lie down head to toe. That's how long that snake is!

Did you know
that some snakes can fly? They flatten their bellies and then glide from tree to tree.

The strongest

Ants are very small animals but they are incredibly strong. They can lift things that are much bigger and heavier than they are. An ant could easily carry fifty other ants on his back. Can you imagine what it would be like to carry fifty children on your back?

The heaviest

Have you ever tried to lift your dad?
He's probably very heavy.
Well, an elephant is even heavier.
He can weigh as much as
sixty-five fathers.

Did you know that the elephant has the longest nose of all the animals and his ears alone are bigger than you are?

The highest jumper

Do you think of yourself as an enormous giant? Well, you are, at least compared to the flea. This little animal lives in the fur of animals like dogs, monkeys and giraffes. When a flea bites, it itches horribly. That is how a tiny animal can make the life of a much bigger one miserable.

Fleas may be small but they can jump really high. A flea could easily jump over this book if you hold it upright. Now try to imagine the size of this book when you are as tiny as that. If you could jump as high as a flea can, you would be able to jump over tall buildings with the greatest of ease.

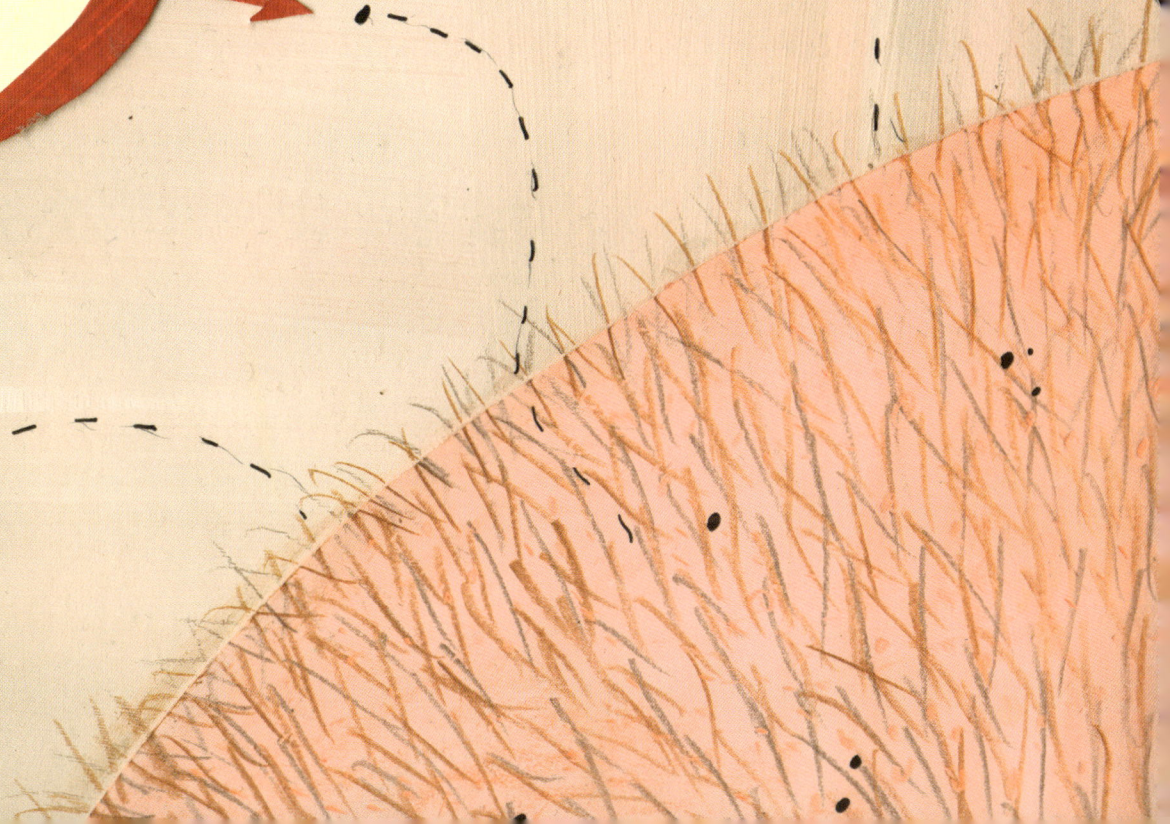

REAL SIZE

The fastest

The fastest flying animal in the world is the falcon. This bird of prey hunts other birds by diving from a great height. Falcons dive so fast they go faster than a racing car.

Do you like to race? You couldn't beat this animal. Cheetahs are the fastest of all the land animals. When they go hunting, they can run as fast as a car drives on the highway. But they can only keep that pace up for a minute or so. Then they get tired and have to stop.

Did you know
some dragonflies
are faster than a lion?
And that some dogs
run faster than a tiger?

 =

falcon = racing car

 =

cheetah = car

 =

lion = truck

 =

cat = motorbike

mouse = bike

The slowest

The slowest animal in the world is the snail. Try running around your yard.
It will probably only take a few minutes. But it'll take a snail the whole day
to do the same thing.

The most dangerous

Crocodiles are dangerous animals. They eat fish, birds and other animals. When they go out hunting, they disappear almost entirely underwater. That way they can sneak up on their prey and pull them underwater before the prey can try to get away.

Other dangerous animals are polar bears, buffalos, hippopotami and snakes. But you don't have to be afraid of those animals. In fact, they might be even more afraid of you. You see, for animals, humans are the most dangerous creatures in the world.

Lions and tigers are also dangerous. When they hunt, they quietly stalk through the high grass and then pounce on their prey.

A lot of people believe that sharks are dangerous, but they are not so bad. Sharks prefer eating fish and seals. If a shark attacks a person, it's probably because it mistook the human for a seal.

Did you know some people like crocodile sandwiches? And others like a soup made of delicious shark?

Whales often come to the surface to breathe. Sometimes they blow enormous fountains of water into the air. The fountain, which is called a spout, can be higher than a house.

Have you ever seen a crocodile brush his teeth? Probably not. Ancient historians told of a little bird that picks the leftovers from between the crocodile's teeth. The story goes that the crocodile doesn't eat the bird because he appreciates having clean teeth.

Did you know the ocean is deeper in some places than the highest mountain in the world?

Here are some amazing animals at home. Take a look!

Polar bears live at the North Pole where it is bitterly cold. Because their fur is white, polar bears can blend in with the snow and can easily sneak up on a seal or other prey without being noticed.

The sea is swarming with fish, jellyfish, little lobsters and other aquatic animals. We call a big sea an ocean.

The most beautiful

Mirror, mirror on the wall, who is the most beautiful of them all?
That is, without a doubt, the peacock. Look at all those beautiful colors!
The male peacock tries to impress the female. He wears a little crown and
if he puts his tail feathers upright a magnificent fan of colored feathers
appears behind him. That's how he says: I am the most beautiful creature
of them all.

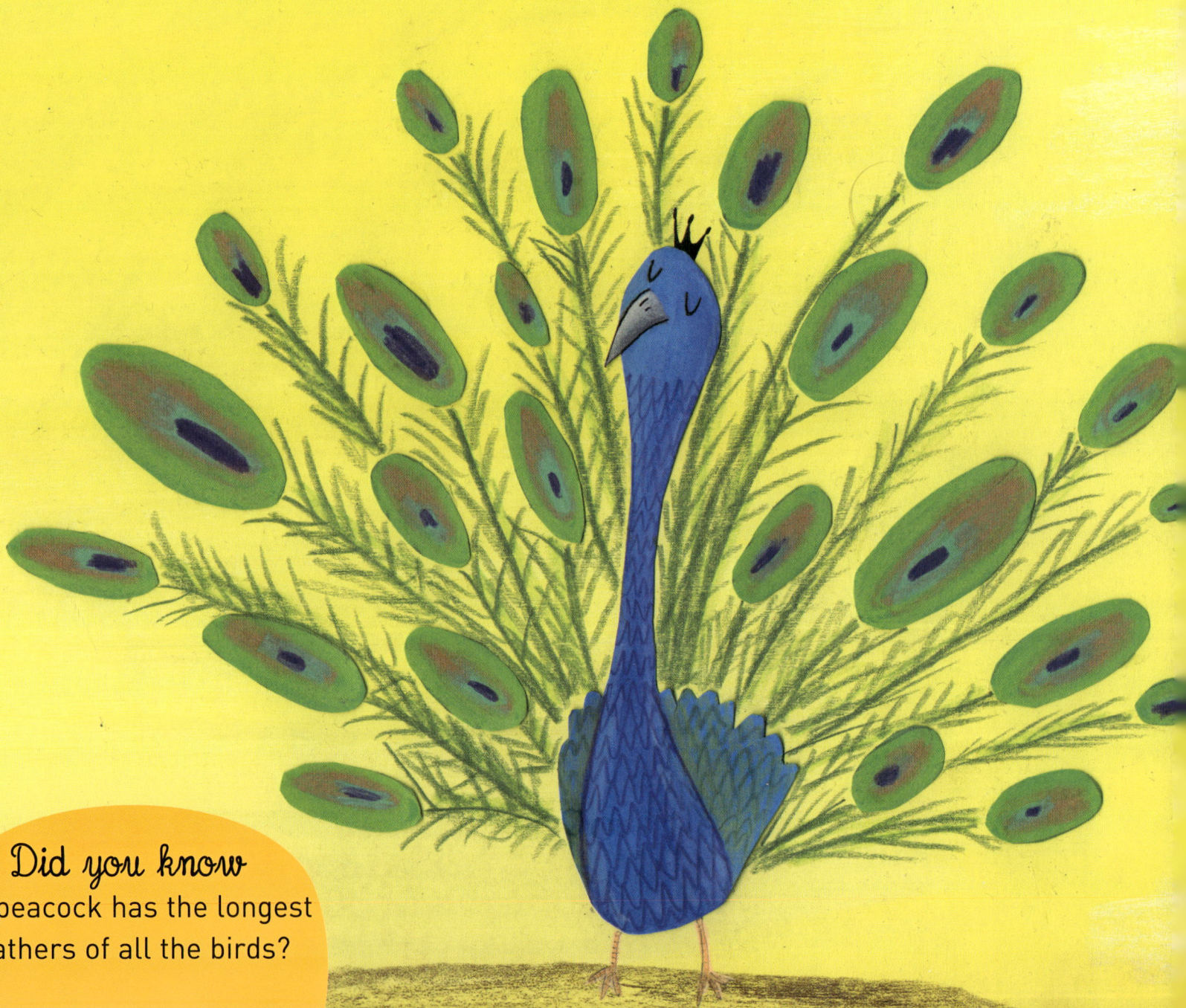

Did you know
the peacock has the longest
feathers of all the birds?

The oldest

Of all the animals tortoises live the longest.
They can live to be a hundred and fifty years old.
Tortoises don't get old like humans do,
they just keep growing and getting
bigger and bigger.

Did you know
some tortoises grow so big
you can ride on their backs?

The youngest

Mayflies live much shorter lives. Some people call them
dayflies because that's the longest they live – one day.
Maybe that's why mayflies are always in such a hurry.
They don't even take time to eat!

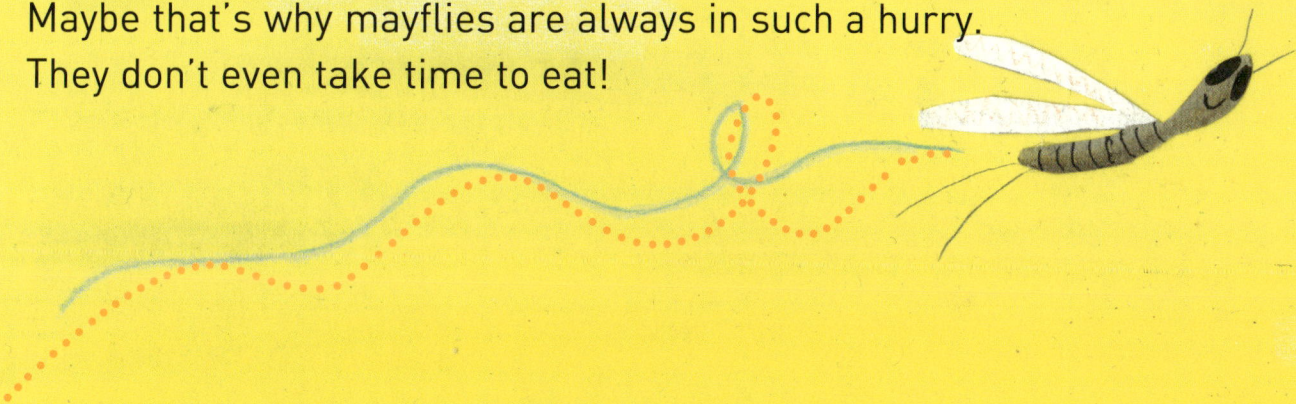

Lots of animals live in the forest.
In warmer countries, it is often humid in
the forests and they are called rainforests.
Rainforests are almost always noisy because
there are whistling, fluttering, squeaking,
growling, grumbling, roaring and screaming
animals everywhere.

The savannah is a large
grassy plain. During the
day it is extremely hot.
Elephants, giraffes, lions,
cheetahs and lots of other
sun-loving animals live
on the savannah.

Turtles live both on land and in water. They are excellent swimmers. The mother turtle lays eggs on land and buries them carefully in the sand.

LOOK AT THIS STRANGE FISH. IT LOOKS LIKE A GIANT PUDDING HEAD.

The strangest

There are a lot of strange animals on the planet. What do you think of a fish with a little lamp on its head? This fish lives very deep under the sea where it is dark all the time. Little fish swim towards the light, and then: snap! The little fish is dinner!

Have you ever seen a stick with feet? No? Well then you should definitely take a closer look at the stick insect – also called the walking stick. This little animal has a very clever trick. If it seems like another animal might eat him, he stays absolutely still and pretends to be a stick. Because sticks aren't half as good to eat as insects are, the stick insect is left alone by the hungry predator.

hey

hi

Guess who?

I have a beak and paws like a duck.
I have a fur as soft as a mole's.
I have the tail of a beaver.
And I lay eggs. Guess who?

Correct ... I am the platypus!

ME? FUNNY LOOKING?
TAKE A LOOK IN THE MIRROR!

'A Kiss from Rabbit'

1. Rabbit walks through the forest. It is a beautiful day.

2. A bit further on Rabbit sees Giraffe. "Hi Giraffe," Rabbit says. "I am so glad you are my friend." "Why?" Giraffe asks

3. "You are the tallest animal in the forest. You can reach the top of the tree and always pick the best apples for me." Rabbit gives Giraffe a kiss.

4. Soon after, she sees Elephant. "Hi Elephant," Rabbit says. "I am so glad you are my friend." "Why?" Elephant asks.

5. "You are the strongest animal in the forest. You chase away all the scary animals." Rabbit gives Elephant a kiss.

Along comes Cheetah. "Hi Cheetah," Rabbit says. "I am so glad you are my friend." "Why?" Cheetah asks.

7.

"Because you are the fastest animal of all. You always deliver my letters so quickly." Cheetah gets a kiss.

A bit further Rabbit comes across Squirrel lying in the grass. "Hi Squirrel," Rabbit says. "I am so glad you are my friend." "Why?" Squirrel wants to know.

"You are so soft and are so nice to cuddle up against. You are the softest of them all." Rabbit gives Squirrel a kiss.

9.

Rabbit is sad. Giraffe is the tallest one. Elephant is the strongest one. Cheetah is the fastest one. Squirrel is the softest one. *What about me? Am I special too?* She wonders sadly.

Along come Giraffe, Elephant, Cheetah and Squirrel. "Hi Rabbit," they call cheerfully. "We are so very happy that you are our friend!

11. You are the very sweetest friend in the whole wide world."

In the animal train

Come sit in the animal train
and help us sing a refrain
It's all quite melodious,
so please come and join us
Aboard the animal train!

The impalas sing lala
The boas sing o-a
The monkeys sing oo-ee
The beetles sing oobla dee
The snails sing scales
The stoats hum notes
The kudus tap
The turtles snap
Aboard the animal train!

There are so many animals who share the world with us.
There are so many animals who are quite marvellous!
Some of them are really big and really wide or tall.
Some are so very little you don't see them at all.
Some live in the mountains, some live in the trees,
Some fly way up in the sky, some swim the seven seas
There are so many creatures you can learn about.
There are so many creatures, way more than you can count!

Make your own sock puppet

This is what you need:

An old sock

Felt in various colors

Construction paper in various colors

Two buttons or beads

Wool

A pair of scissors, pins, a needle and thread

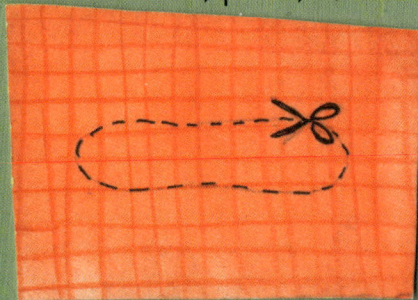

1.

2.

3.

This is what you do:

1. Cut the sock around the front to make a mouth.
2. Use a piece of felt or construction paper for the inside of the mouth.
   Cut out an oval that's about double the size of the mouth. Fold it in half.
3. Pin the felt or paper to the sock, then sew it to the sock as shown in the picture.
4. Your puppet now needs hair, eyes, ears, and a nose. For the hair you use wool.
   For the eyes you can use buttons, beads or a piece of felt. The ears and nose can
   be made out of felt or construction paper

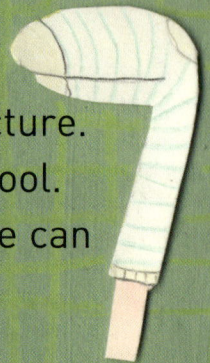

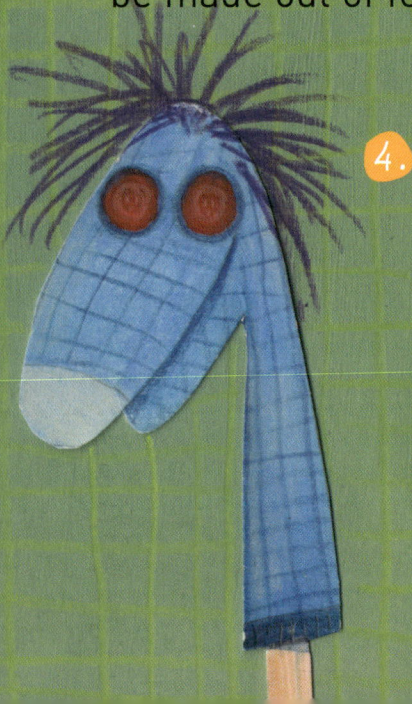

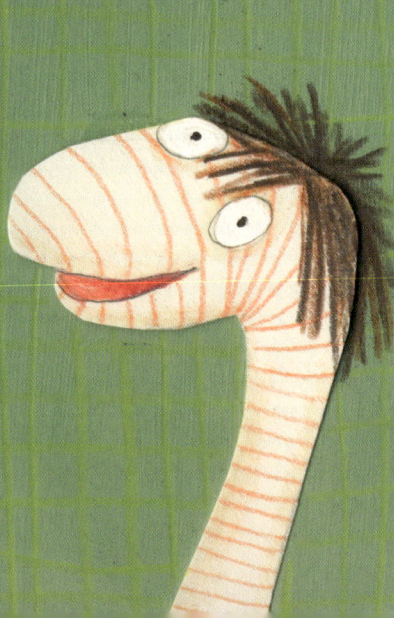

4.

What crazy animals!

Animal quiz

1. Which one of these is the fastest animal?

2. What do sharks love to eat?

3. What is the biggest animal on earth?

4. Which animal has the longest nose?

5. How tall can a giraffe be?

6. What kind of animal is this?

7. Which animal can live the longest?

8. Can fish fly?

9. How long is the longest snake?

10. How high can a flea jump?